Other works by Nicole Suzanne Brown
Non- fiction -
Passing through Time - Conversations with the Other Side

The Creativity Workbook

The Wee Little Book of The Awesome

The Meaning of Feathers

The Meaning of Numbers

Go LIVE like a PRO - 18page digital Workbook.

Be a Freakin' Lighthouse! - 22page digital Workbook

From Overwhelm to Awesome - (free) 18page digital Workbook

Fiction -
Pride

Outback Mistress 2020

Phoenix 2019

Home Grown 2019

On the Job 2021

For further information, updates, pre-ordering & awesomeness email Nicole at nickibtv1@gmail.com

ACKNOWLEDGMENTS

Firstly, to my gorgeous wife Anne-Marie. The Universe moved Heaven & Earth for us to meet and fall in love. I wished on every Star for years (as you did yourself) and I couldn't imagine ever being so happy, loved, and living my life with my Best Friend. I love you to the Moon and Back.

To Mum and Dad, you always lift me up, allow me to soar, support, and nurture, and are my shoulders to lean on when life seems unfair. You are the best parents a spiritual girl like me could have. You kick my butt when it needs kicking and kiss my cheek when I'm feeling vulnerable. I love you both so much.

The Meaning of Numbers   Nicole Suzanne Brown

Copyright © 2018 Nicole Suzanne Brown
All rights reserved.

The moral rights of the author have been asserted. All rights reserved. No part of this book may be reproduced by any mechanical, photographic or electronic process, or in the form of a photographic recording; nor be stored in a retrieval system, transmitted or otherwise be copied for public or private use, other than for 'fair use' as brief quotations embodied in articles and reviews, without prior written permission of the publisher.

The author of this book does not dispense medical advice or prescribe the use of any technique as a form of treatment for physical or medical problems without the advice of a physician, either directly or indirectly.

The intent of the author is only to offer information of a general nature to help you in your quest for emotional and spiritual wellbeing. In the event you use any of the information in this book for yourself, which is your constitutional right, the author and the publisher assume no responsibility for your actions.

The Meaning of Numbers   Nicole Suzanne Brown

First Edition 2018

Published in Australia by Spiritual Wisdom Publishing

Book design by Spiritual Wisdom Publishing
© 2018 Nicole Suzanne Brown
National Library of Australia

DEDICATION

To Jay,

For being my muse throughout the writing of this book.

And for reminding me constantly that life is way too short to be stressing about the small stuff, and that miracles occur with every breath we take.

Contents

ACKNOWLEDGMENTS...4
DEDICATION..5
The Meaning of Numbers - foreward 9
The Spiritual and Physical Meaning of Numbers:........10
If the number appeared on your LEFT: 11
If the number appeared on your RIGHT:..................12
How you can use this book 13
The Meaning of Number 1 17
Physical Meaning 18
Spiritual Meaning...19
The Meaning of Number 2 20
Physical Meaning 21
Spiritual Meaning...22
The Meaning of Number 3 23
Physical Meaning 24
Spiritual Meaning...25
The Meaning of Number 4 26
Physical Meaning 27
Spiritual Meaning...28
The Meaning of Number 5 29
Physical Meaning 31
Spiritual Meaning...32
The Meaning of Number 6 33
Physical Meaning 34
Spiritual Meaning...35
The Meaning of Number 7 36
Physical Meaning 37

Spiritual Meaning	38
The Meaning of Number 8	39
Physical Meaning	41
Spiritual Meaning	42
The Meaning of Number 9	43
Physical Meaning	44
Spiritual Meaning	45
The Meaning of Number 0	46
Physical Meaning	47
Spiritual Meaning	48
What do double numbers mean?	49
The Meaning of Master Number 11	50
Physical Meaning	51
Spiritual Meaning	52
The Meaning of Master Number 22	53
Physical Meaning	55
Spiritual Meaning	56
The Meaning of Master Number 33	58
Physical Meaning	60
Spiritual Meaning	61
Read the meaning of Number 3 for more insight	61
The Meaning of Months	62
January - 01 energy	63
February - 02 energy	66
March - 03 energy	68
April - 04 energy	70
May - 05 energy	72
June - 06 energy	74

July - 07 energy 76
August - 08 energy 79
September - 09 energy 82
October - 10 energy 84
November - 11 energy 87
December - 12 energy 89
One last thing… 92
Chapter 9. About Nicole: 94
Other works by Nicole Suzanne Brown 95
The Meaning of Feathers 95
Reviews for The Meaning of Feathers 97
The Creativity Workbook - kindle only 98
Passing through Time 100
Reviews for Passing Through Time: 101
Chapter one 104
Passing Through Time 104
Conversations with the Other Side 104
First Conversation with Jason 106
Jason's Experience 109
Fiction novels also by Nicole Suzanne Brown 123
Outback Mistress (2019) 123
CHAPTER 1. 123

The Meaning of Numbers - foreward

I was never any good at maths. I never understood the whole x + y = 5 stuff and the more my teacher would try to explain it the more I wondered why he thought those shirts went with those pants. Looking back on it, nothing in high school really did make sense.

It wasn't until much later in my mid-twenties when I came across the book "The Life You Were Born To Live" by Dan Millman that I finally GOT the meaning of numbers. Suddenly, the meaning of numbers made sense to me! I could not only add, subtract and divide like a 5year old math prodigy, I could SEE numbers and the energy of those equations around people, and KNOW that that is WHY they do what they do. I understood that the Universe was entirely made up of mathematical equations and series of 1's & 0's that now that I understand what the number 1 and the number 0 mean, blows me away each and every day.

It was like the key to a lock I never knew I always had to open.

We are born with specific numbers and energies already established in our lives with our birth dates, this is true. But did you know that the meaning of numbers could be significant in not only your relationships, but your career, and where you choose to live?

The Spiritual and Physical Meaning of Numbers:

So is there a spiritual and physical meaning to seeing particular numbers over and over again? I believe there is. There are so many messages involved when a number is gifted to you, and one of the most important is acknowledging if the message is a Spiritual meaning or a Physical meaning.

In other words, when you saw the number did you find it on the left hand side of your body or the right hand side of your body?

If the number appeared on your *LEFT*:

This indicates a very strong SPIRITUAL message for you. Your higher self has brought you to this very moment to receive the message you are about to receive. Understand that this message is for your SOUL, your spiritual self, the shadow side of your nature, the dreamer and the lover within you.

The message is being sent to you FROM YOUR soul TO YOUR soul. You planned this moment in life. You planned to receive this sign, this message right now at this moment to move you into the best place your life could be. Acknowledge the message with pure unconditional love.

Read the Spiritual Meaning and Affirmation section in each of the numbers you feel connected to.

If the number appeared on your **RIGHT**:

This indicates a very strong PHYSICAL message for you. The Universe, God, Spiritual Guides or those of our loved ones that have passed before us, are gifting you a message so that your physical side, your body, mind and emotional side can heal, move on from the past and step forward to a brighter, healthier, happier and joy-filled future.

Read the Spiritual Meaning and Affirmation section in each of the numbers you feel connected to.

How you can use this book

Numbers are such an integral part of our every day life.

From our birthdate, to the house number where we choose to live , they follow us wherever we go.

Have you always noticed a particular number occurring in your life?

Is there always a house number where you have chosen to live?

What's your favourite number?

Everyone has one.

You can use this book as a guide and a reference.

For example, today is the 22nd Sept.

I can read the meaning of the Number 2, the Master number 22 & the Month Number 09 to receive an accurate reading of today's energy.

My birthdate is 02 -11. I can then read the meaning of the Number 0, the Number 2 & the Master Number 11.

If today's date was the 14th. You can read the Number 1 then the Number 4.

If however the number you see constantly is the number 41, the reading would be Number 4 first, then the Number 1.

Whichever number appears first is the most dominant number.

Now, let's delve into what each Number, Master Number (11, 22 & 33) & Month represents.

The Meaning of Numbers – What do single numbers mean?

I truly believe that Universal messages come in to our lives, in the most unexpected ways. What better way is there than a lovely unexpected message and gifting from above?

So, what is the meaning behind these messages? Is there any significance at all in not only the value of the number but where we find it?

I believe there is. I believe that everything around us is a message from the Universe, God, and Spirit. I believe that we have drawn these numbers to us like Universal signposts, to jog our memories, to trigger an emotion, to understand the Universe and how, where and WHY we fit in to it. I believe this is what is meant by 'we are not alone', and 'we are always guiding you'. I believe if we truly looked within, worked out our emotions BEFORE we acted upon them, that we wouldn't need any outside influences to guide us. We have given ourselves the gift of remembrance. And within each number that we continue to see over and over again, that is our Souls way of setting us back on a path we may have diverted from OR more than likely, given us a clear insight of how far we have come and how proud we should be of ourselves.

We after all are ONE with EACH OTHER.

ALL IS ONE IS ONE.

But, until that moment that we truly listen to our own inner voice, inner guidance, let's celebrate the fact that we have planned this message, and received it loud and clear.

Let's look closer at each number and what it represents to you.

The Meaning of Number 1

The number 1 represents singularity, independence, focus and at times stubbornness.

If you constantly see the number 1, the Universe is asking you to remain focused on your task at hand. Be not swayed by another's judgement or criticism.

There may be times when you feel you are alone, and not being noticed.

Ask yourself why you feel you need the approval of others? Do you exist for them?

Let go of the need to be 'seen' and really FEEL the connection back to your heart center.

You were born strong and independent for a reason.

Be sure in the knowledge that you are a born leader.

Physical Meaning

It's time to stop procrastinating. You are being asked to truly find the strength inside you to move forward in your life and leave the past behind you. The lesson here is movement. Find a new way to move your body physically and emotionally. Dance, sing, laugh. Connect with your 'self' again and ask yourself what makes you happy, then DO THAT.

Affirmation "My body and mind are clear and free. I draw inspiration and creativity from the Universe to express myself with strength and honesty. I am loved. I am strong. I am safe".

Spiritual Meaning

It's time to find the faith in yourself and the connecting with the Universe. You are being asked to trust and KNOW that the Universe now has cleared your path towards a brighter, happier future. A cleansing has taken place. Meditate. Pray. Be Grateful and filled with Grace. Give thanks for your past and gratitude for your future.

Affirmation "I am one with the Universe. The Universe flows through me and for me. My pathway is clear. My future is bright. I am exactly where I need to be".

The Meaning of Number 2

The number 2 represents duality, communication, relationship with self and at times a strong need to feel part of a larger community.

If you constantly see the number 2, the Universe is asking you to see the larger picture.

Are you wanting to be part of something bigger? Is there a need to start communicating your needs clearly and precisely?

Ask yourself - are you being not only listened to, but really heard?

Is there a need to speak up where before you remained quiet?

Your voice and words are your strongest asset.

The Universe is asking you to use your words wisely.

Like a writer that can cut with a pen, your words can hold a sting in them that will last for eons.

Know that there is great power in the words you choose.

Choose them wisely.

Physical Meaning

You are being asked to remain true to yourself through your communication with others. There is a situation that you have become involved in that needs clarification. Speak with your heart, not with your past. Your words can heal or hurt. Be aware of WHO you are speaking about. Is it with kindness? If not, ask yourself why not? Why do you feel you need to be powerful over another? Remember, at times, silence is more powerful than words could ever express. If you do need to speak, connect with your heart center.

Affirmation "My voice is my guide. I channel my words through the Universe and speak only with love, kindness and gratitude. I think before I speak. I trust in the power of silence.

Spiritual Meaning

You are being guided to connect with your spiritual voice. You are a powerful leader. Trust that you have the right words at the right time. Your voice calms others and can soothe past hurts. Is there a way you can bring your words to help heal? Trust your intuition.

Affirmation "My intuition is my guiding force. I trust that I am exactly where I need to be. My voice is powerful and my mind is clear. My words heal".

The Meaning of Number 3

The number 3 represents Trilogy and Faith.

Faith in a higher presence yes, but most importantly, faith in your own path, your own self.

It is time now to give TO yourself, THEN to others.

The number 3 also represents money and wealth. Now, wealth could manifest as either abundance OR knowledge.

Ask yourself, are you giving your wealth away?

If you constantly see the number 3, the Universe is asking you to BELIEVE in your 'self'.

Have faith in the life path you have chosen (or about to choose).

Be confident that the Universe is behind you 100%. Know that you will be looked after financially and abundantly.

Be aligned with the wealth of your KNOWLEDGE as well as your monetary energy. Be sure to align yourself with what you are WORTH. Knowledge is a very, very powerful energy to be aligned with. Be sure you are not giving yours away for free.

Physical Meaning

You are being asked to be open to abundance from all sources. An unexpected win-fall is coming. You are being gifted by the Universe. Be TRUE to YOURSELF. You are being reminded that your physical body needs to be fuelled with high energy foods and water (vegetables, fruit etc). Feed your temple so your energy becomes high. Laugh and celebrate. Your life is about to change for the better.

Affirmation "I am so loved and so grateful. Money comes to me daily in unexpected ways. I accept all abundance gratefully. I am energised with life. I trust the Universe & love my life".

Spiritual Meaning

You are being reminded to have Faith in your SELF. The Universe is guiding you to your next adventure. Trust you are exactly where you need to be. Allow yourself to be guided. If it scares you, do it. Go within and become in love with your true self again. Find that child within. Laugh, dance and sing. Share your story. Trust in your own path.

Affirmation "I am so grateful that my path is clear and open. I let go and trust my self to take the steps I need. I love where my life is heading and am excited each and every day".

The Meaning of Number 4

The number 4 represents building a strong foundation and balance.

Balance in all aspects of your life. Spiritually, Physically, Emotionally and Mentally.

Every aspect of your life needs to have a strongly built foundation for which to grow from.

If you constantly see the number 4, the Universe is asking you to take time in getting your own self 'right'. Is there an aspect of yourself that you need to work on and make stronger before you forge ahead?

Take notice of your sleeping and eating patterns.

Are you giving your body the best foundation for optimal health?

Is there an aspect in your career you need to work on before applying for a promotion or change of venue?

Be aware of where you can nurture and build from in your own life.

This is the time of building.

Do not be rushed.

Physical Meaning

You are being guided to stay strong in a situation with your family. Your family foundations have been rocked, and family members are looking to you to set it right. Stay firm in your convictions and speak from your heart. Placing your right hand on your heart and left on your solar plexus (belly button) when you speak will allow you to keep your strength and inner power. You are loved and safe.

Affirmation "I am strong. The Universe guides me with my strength. I am always filled with gratitude. I am safe. I am loved".

Spiritual Meaning

There is a situation surrounding you which will test the strength of your own personal faith. You are being asked to look within to find what you have let go off in your own belief systems. You have turned a blind eye to injustices that you could have stood up to. There is an area of your life that you feel uneasy about due to not standing strong in your own morals. Look within. Clear your conscious. Make it right.

Affirmation "I allow the Universe to guide me to a place of change. Change is powerful. I am safe in change. My path is clear. I speak with honesty, love and kindness".

The Meaning of Number 5

The number 5 represents freedom from your own limitations, and the energy of "Fight or Flight".

If you constantly see the number 5, the Universe is asking you to focus on where you are holding limiting beliefs.

Are you stopping yourself from starting a relationship because you feel too fat, too broke, too sad, too eccentric?

Have you placed yourself in a situation you feel you are 'stuck' in and can never leave?

Have you been living in such fear of change and the unknown it is literally all you now know?

Where in your life have you imprisoned yourself?

Does your temper get the better of you?

Are you constantly in fear of ridicule, isolation and live in a constant state of anxiety?

Stop. Take a deep breath.

Know that you are loved, that you are safe, that you can say no, or yes, or not now or I have to go.

Allow yourself the chance to choose differently.

Be safe in the knowledge that you will never make a wrong decision.

The Meaning of Numbers	Nicole Suzanne Brown

Step away from the box you put yourself in.
Reach out and ask for help.

Physical Meaning

You are being guided to notice where your energy is being blocked. Joint pains and aches may occur through the inability to move forward from your past. Seek counsel. Be aware that you have gotten through the worst of a situation and now it is time to free yourself from guilt and fear. Breathe in light. Breathe out light. Visualise your body filled with light from the inside out. Notice where in your body it is not flowing freer. Forgive yourself. And love who you have become.

Affirmation "I walk freely through life with ease. My future is bright. The Universe protects me with each step I take and every decision I make. I am filled with light. I am safe".

Spiritual Meaning

You are being asked to recognise that you are carrying the weight of your families decisions and grievances for far too long. It is time to step forward in your own power, your own path in life. Let go of what no longer serves you. This is your life, your time. Allow yourself to be happy. You deserve the best in life. Trust that this is your right.

Affirmation "My life is filled with love, laughter, happiness and joy. New adventures excite me. I say yes to change. I am free to make my own decisions. I love my life".

The Meaning of Number 6

The number 6 represents family and friendships/relationships.

If you constantly see the number 6, the Universe is asking you to connect back to your heart center.

Have you recently lost a family member/friend that you felt your heart would be broken forever?

Be still and know that you are loved.

You are being led back to your heart center so that you can heal, you can mend and you can be loved.

Allow others to look after you.

Be aware of your need to be in control.

Step back. Trust and understand that this is your rest time now. Everything is as it should be.

There may be a feeling of concern or frustration around a Mother or Father figure.

Go into those feelings and be aware that what you are feeling is your own frustration in acceptance and belonging.

Physical Meaning

You are being asked to forgive your Mother. There is a situation that needs to be healed and forgiven. Let go of all judgement and disappointment around a home/workplace situation. Nurture yourself. Give yourself time to grieve and heal. It's ok to not be ok. Give yourself permission to feel the emotion then let everything but love go.

Affirmation "*I am exactly where I need to be right now to heal. Love surrounds me every day. I forgive. I love. I am nurtured by life. I am ok*".

Spiritual Meaning

You are being asked to forgive your Father. It is time to let go of fear and anger. You are being guided to a place of strength. Stand strong in your power. Be gentle with yourself. It's ok to not know all the answers. Allow yourself the time to find what you are passionate about in life. Explore new avenues.

Affirmation "I allow myself the gift of time. I am guided to where I need to be. My life path is clear. I am excited about the future. My passion for life excites me. I am protected".

The Meaning of Number 7

The number 7 represents life experience.

If you constantly see the number 7, the Universe is hinting that you are about to go on an adventure, be it physical travel or spiritually (astral).

There may be times when you feel you are constantly hitting brick walls in your relationships and career and the Universe is allowing you now to take stock of your past experiences, learn from them.

Move on.

There may be times when you are surrounded always by people and feel the need to find a new adventure to go to.

Do not let boredom rule your life.

Stay put. Breathe in.

Ask the Universe what you need to learn from this experience right now?

The answers may surprise you.

Physical Meaning

You are being guided to dream BIG. The Universe has a plan for you that you need to trust. Take the promotion. Say yes to the blind date. Find the power within yourself to know that you no longer make the same mistakes. Forgive your past. Update your passport. Buy the shoes.

Affirmation "I wake each day ready for a new adventure. Exciting opportunities come to me every day. I say yes to adventures. My future is so bright. I embrace change and am free to travel".

Spiritual Meaning

You are being asked to recognise a pattern in your life that you need to learn from, and let go of. It is time to move on and start a fresh. Unchain yourself from a situation in the past that has held you back from reach your true potential. Be brave. Let it all go. Start afresh.

Affirmation "My future is filled with amazing possibilities. I trust my instincts. My intuition guides me. I have faith in myself and my future. I am surrounded by love".

The Meaning of Number 8

The number 8 represents Universal balance in all things.

It is the Universal symbol of the Alpha & Omega.

The Beginning and The End.

Karma. Infinity.

It is the never ending energy of rebirth and death.

If you constantly see the number 8, the Universe is asking you to remain vigilant in your thoughts, words and deeds.

Be aware of the ENERGY of what you are putting out to the world.

Are you constantly in the energy of blame or acceptance? Taking or Giving?

Your life may feel like it is going through a major upheaval.

Let it come. There will always be rebirth after death. A rainbow after the storm. Let go of what no longer serves you.

Start again.

Start anew.
Become connected with all things, everywhere.
Move as if you were one with the Universe.
Allow the Universe to guide you.

Physical Meaning

You are being asked to step back from a situation with a friend. Recognise where your energy is flowing to. Is it for the good of all or only for some? Balance in all areas of your life is needed. Drink Water. Let go of the past. Flow.

Affirmation "My life flows effortlessly and easily. I am balanced in every area of my life. My energy flows freely. I sleep peacefully and wake fully rested".

Spiritual Meaning

You are being guided to recognise that the life you have been living is not your own. It is time to let go fully of the past. You have done all you can. Move forward with ease and grace. Balance your finances. Notice where your energy is flowing to. Let go of bad influences and influencers.

Affirmation "I am free to be me. My life is filled with amazing new opportunities. I am balanced in all areas of my life. My future is bright. I am happy, joyful and grateful for all that I have now and in the future".

The Meaning of Number 9

The number 9 represents completion.

Now in some cases with the number 9 it can mean that you have felt that everything is always up to you to finalise, you are the one to end things, move on, let go of, take control of.

If you constantly see the number 9, the Universe is asking you to have the strength to delegate.

If you do not, there will be the energy of overwhelm and frustration.

Is there a task or relationship you need to finalise for you to move forward.

The Universe is reminding you to tie up all loose ends.

A stepping into a new role is happening.

No need to bring your past into the future.

Physical Meaning

You are being asked to stop. Breathe. You have done enough. It is time to rest. Recuperate. Dream of your new adventures. Let go of what has happened. Ask for help everyday. Delegate. Let go of control. You are completely safe in every decision you make.

Affirmation "My life is my own. I am free to make choices. My happiness is my own. I am loved. I celebrate every success. My future is brighter. My mind is still and calm".

Spiritual Meaning

You are being guided to sit still and give thanks for what has happened in the past that led you to this moment, right now. Breathe away any tension and see yourself moving forward through your day with strength, surrounded by happiness and laughter. It's ok to cry. Your past is forgiven.

Affirmation "All that I am, and all that I do is ok for me. My life is filled with happiness and laughter. My life path is now clear. I am surrounded by light. I am protected and looked after. Others help me daily".

The Meaning of Number 0

The number 0 represents Inner Gifts and Universal Knowledge.

You may notice that you are beginning to focus on the number 0 more and more as we go through this millennium towards the next.

The number 0 is so powerful in itself that it holds all Universal knowledge and power.

If you constantly see the number 0, the Universe is asking you to allow your Inner Gift and Universal Knowledge to come forth.

You were born for a purpose. It is time now to share your gifts and knowledge with humanity.

The more you ignore this energy the more power you give the ignorant.

Know that you were given this gifting and knowledge for the ultimate purpose - to 'move' the collective consciousness. You were born to make others feel more, be more, love more, laugh more, think more, strive for better, be the best.

You are a gift from God, the Universe and Everything.

Physical Meaning

You are being asked to recognise how truly magnificent you are. You are born to move others to their highest potential. Let go of fear of ridicule. Embrace your gifts. Share them with the World. Write. Dance. Sing. Create and celebrate. Life is yours for the taking. Your life is now a clean slate.

Affirmation "My power is in my voice. My power is in my passion for life. I am surrounded by loving creative friends and family. My body is fuelled with healthy foods. I am a Teacher. I embrace my destiny with an open heart and mind".

Spiritual Meaning

You are being guided to recognise your true Spiritual Gifts. Time to trust your intuition. Your gift is giving to you by the Universe. It is time to tap in what is buried inside you and allow it to break free. Like a Phoenix you will rise from the ashes of your past. Be still and be guided to where you next need to be. Travel is in your near future.

Affirmation "I trust my intuitive self. I am always in the right place at exactly the right time. I allow the Universe to guide me. My life is filled with adventure. I embrace change. I am the change".

What do double numbers mean?

In many areas of our lives we are directed to a certain place and time to acknowledge our ancestral roots be it in this life or the many that we are living on other dimensions (read Passing through Time - Conversations with the Other Side for more clarification)

In numerology there is such a thing as Master Numbers.

These numbers are 11, 22, 33 & so on.

The Number 11 is such a number. As I wrote in the previous chapter - the Number 1 is powerfully linked with leadership and rule. Independence and steadfastness. Couple with another number 1 these energies once powerful are now magnetic in every thought, word and deed.

The following pages are more in depth in explanation to show you the importance of the energy of the Master Number vibration.

The Meaning of Master Number 11

The Master Number 11 brings with it great responsibility.

You are connected to the Earth as are we all, but, you have an undeniable questioning thirst to learn and understand why things happen, and why in a particular order.

Stars and the Moon hold an incredible power over you.

As a child you were sometimes found outside just staring up at the night sky, even being so fascinated as to become interested in Astronomy later in life.

You gravitate to one star in particular, that being that of Orion's belt.

Instinctively you are aware of that particular constellations power and the immense responsibility the planet holds in the overall wellbeing of the Universe.

Physical Meaning

You are being asked to be aware that the Universe is guiding you to remember your ancestral path, and take notice of what you are directing your energies too. Are you feeling powerful or power-filled?

The latter meaning, has there been an instance in your life where you have felt the need to control a situation or person? Are you dreams coming into reality? Are you fingertips tingly, you feel a short buzzing in your left ear and a dull headache on the top of your head that you cannot seem to shift?

All these symptoms are leading you to an awakening. Think of it as a personal signpost that you yourself put in place, so that you would know when you arrived at a certain place and time, that you were to stop, and truly listen to your inner voice, those instincts that are telling you to be still, be guided.

Affirmation "I trust that my intuition is guiding me. I am focused. I am filled with a greater understanding of the Universe. My mind is clear. I am in control of my surroundings. My throat and voice is strong. People are drawn to my kindness. I am aware I am not alone".

Spiritual Meaning

You are being asked to understand the link with those that have the ability to talk the talk. You are wise beyond your years and able to convey trust and an ability to attract wealth, power and knowledge to them at an incredible rate.

Your thirst for knowledge can be closely linked with your need to control, and sometimes overpower. Your energy is now clear to draw to you true love and true happiness. You are surrounded always by loved ones past and present. You are being presented a gift.

Affirmation "I allow the Universe to guide me to a place of kindness and understanding of my true Spiritual self. I trust my intuition. My intuition is my guide. I allow the Universe to flow through me and from me. I am always looked after".

Read the meaning of Number 1 for more insight.

The Meaning of Master Number 22

A funny thing happened to us on the way to the new millennium or The Naughties as some of us Aussies like to call it. A shift occurred around us, within the elements of the space time continuum, but, and most importantly, a shift began to awaken WITHIN us.

Within this shift itself was a power energy that has lain dormant for many ancestral years, until our DNA brought with it a remembrance of memories, dreams that became tangible and something to strive for.

We stepped out of the industrial age where we needed to work hard for less, and began to question why we were working in the first place.

Lifestyle began to replace working life, and we felt a strong pull to set out on our own. & join others who felt the same.

Long lost friends and lovers where reunited, and our need to learn from our own mistakes and let them go forever became our number one goal.

Why this shift and why then?

Why did it happen?

Because for almost 2 thousand years (1 – 1999) we all lived in the dimension/state of the 1 energy.

That of leadership and learning, growing and stumbling, and now, albeit rather slowly, we have started shaking off the blinders and begun questioning not why we are here, but the reason of what we are to do, while we are here.

The energy of the Masterful Number 22 is our most powerful ally.

It is community and collective consciousness, communication and commitment.

It is the energy we hold onto when all else fails.

The Omnipotent and the Oppressor all rolled into one.

Physical Meaning

You are being asked to recognise an intricate connection to the world, even though you sometimes do not seem to feel part of IT. Instead you see beyond, you see the potential of life, the dance of energy connecting everyone to everything.

You are a 'high energy' being – in other words, you cannot be held back especially when needing to express yourself. You can be seen as the trouble maker and the rule breaker.

You have the ability to connect others to their life's gifts. You are a teacher AND a scholar, needing to learn more and more about how and why people behave the way they do.

You feel connected to the wind and the ocean currents, the Moon is you ally, the Sun your guide. Water is your power energy, and some may even have a strong fear of water.

If this is the case, it is your own power that you have become fearful of. Your emotional state needs to connect again with your body and exercises using slow breath is ideal (yoga, tai chi etc,).

Affirmation "My body and mind flows as One. I have enough time in the World. I am calm. Everything is happening at exactly the right time".

Spiritual Meaning

You are being reminded to acknowledge your connection to both the Spiritual (Universal) realm and that of the Physical (Earth) realm. You have an unique ability to read others thoughts, and predict patterns in behaviour of those that you feel strongly connected with. Physical touch is very important to you and a feeling of being overwhelmed by others emotions can hamper your instinctual psychic abilities.

You are feeling more of a pull to change your life and lifestyle especially if it is around your birthday. Be sure not to be swayed by others opinions. Your are trusting your instinct.

You are being asked to re-connect with those you feel you can be yourself with. A person that has passed over is close-by and is wanting to gift you with a message. Understand that you need to be comfortable in your surroundings.

You may feel more drawn to the water, and your emotions will be closely tied with the Moon. Your hands may have felt hot and shaky, and this is just the Universe reminding you that you are here for bigger things.

You are the healer.

You are being asked to look at the people you are attracting.

Now is the time to trust your instincts. Find a way to voice your opinion without frustration. A clearing of 'old ways of communicating' may cause irritation to your throat and glands.

Join a group that has a Universal appeal.

Be part of something bigger.

Be aware of your dream state.

You are being guided.

Do not ignore your messages.

Affirmation "I trust the messages that I receive on a daily basis. The Universe and I are One. I acknowledge my Ancestors. I breathe in peace. I surround myself with only the best. I am protected".

Read the meaning of Number 2 for more insight.

The Meaning of Master Number 33

With a continuation of the Master Numbers, we come to Master Number 33.

If 3 was about faith and Universal abundance, Number 33 is that, times ten.

It is said that Jesus birth date added up to a 33, and of course he passed at the age of 33.

You may have found the infant and teenage life tough going. Acceptance of your own gifts, coupled with 'societies' ever changing landscape of more, and must do better, and be the best, will leave you feeling very inadequate indeed.

That is of course until you have reached their late twenties. Then, something changed within you. Your inner strength went into hyper-drive and almost overnight you are faced with a new, stronger (physically & mentally), capable human being.

Where once there was struggle and doubt, now you will have purpose and feel confident.

Purpose and Confident Consciousness explains the number 33 to a tee. You are a very family orientated being, and you bring anyone in from the cold that you deem acceptable.

You need to be discerning however, and if you find you have crossed the wrong side of the path with someone, it would be best to ask for forgiveness and not feel the need to contact them again.

They have moved on long before you even acknowledged there was something to be forgiven for.

Physical Meaning

You are being asked to listen to your inner guidance. A role that you have played with someone has now ended, and it is time to move on to greener pastures. Become aware of the animals and gentle souls that you are surrounding yourself with. Connect with nature again, for it is there you will find your balance. Keep an eye on your finances, and start saving for that 'rainy day', you'll be so glad that did. Have faith that it all works out in the end. Give your strength and voice to a higher calling. Your energy and understanding is much needed. Phone a friend. Don't be a stranger. The Universe is showing you the way. Trust it.

Affirmation "I am loved and protected. I am being guided to a place of love and acceptance. Every day in every way my life is filled with love, joy and happiness".

Spiritual Meaning

You are being guided to seek help from a higher source, whether it be through pray, meditation or counselling. It is now time to let go of the 'small roles' you have put yourself in and start standing up for yourself. Stop living small. You're opinion is needed on an urgent family financial matter. Trust your instincts and do not give in to the will of the small for the good of all. Small financial wins are coming in to your life. You are being asked to have faith in yourself, your instincts and the path you have chosen to take. Understand that this is destined. Breathe and allow things to run there course.

Affirmation "My faith guides me to a place of pure love and acceptance. I wake refreshed. Financial abundance is mine. My bank account is overflowing with wealth. I trust that I am always looked after physically, emotionally and financially".

Read the meaning of Number 3 for more insight

The Meaning of Months

Now that we have established what the meanings of numbers mean let's look deeper in to what each Month of our Calendar represents.

Does each month bring with it it's own energy?

It's own unique lessons & learnings?

I believe they do!

January - 01 energy

The first month of the year always brings with it new & refocused energy.

Do you every wonder why you feel so energised at the start of the year?

Everything seems do-able.

Everything seems in reach.

You're writing your goals, you're setting up your VIBE BOARD™ with all that you want to achieve & you just KNOW you are going to reach every single one of them!

Why?

Because January has the energy of renewal. It has the energy of new possibilities, new growth, new opportunities and a letting go of the past.

It allows us to shake off what we achieved (or didn't achieve) in the past year, and start afresh.

How many of us have started the New Year with the statement "THIS Year is MY Year. Things will be different. I'm ready for it?"

But remember this - What you think about - You bring about it. And what you "bring about" is the *'feeling'* that you are starting the new year with.

January will bring you everything you are desiring, but you need to hold strong to that energy. With the 0 and 1 present, it represents a going within, a resurgence of possible outcomes, and an inner knowing that you have the power all along.

It can also represent an internal struggle of change.

January's energy is Powerful. It is internal. And if you work on yourself, letting go of the old, embracing the new, it will be one of the best Months of the Year, or could break your spirit.

It will be linked with your attitude towards change.

Do you resist it?

Do you feel controlled by it?

Are you ready for it?

What will happen if you receive everything you desire?

How will you feel?

Who will you help?

All these questions are what are asked of you in January.

Let go of that which no longer serves you.

Embrace change. Know you are an incredible Human Being that is destined to be successful in relationships, in wealth, in business and in Life.

Trust your intuition. Dream bigger. Crush your goals.

Affirmation for January

"I embrace change. I attract Wealth, Abundance & love. I am focused and determined. Change brings new adventures to my Life on a day to to day basis. I wake up knowing I am doing exactly what I am here for. My goals are achieved easily and effortlessly. This or Better".

Read Meaning of Number 1 energy for more insight.

February - 02 energy

Now that we have embraced the energy of individualism and change, the Universe provides us with the gift of communication.

There is no coincidence that Valentines Day is linked with this Month as it is the Month of Relationships and communication.

Remembering that the energy of Number 2 is linked with communication, coupling, and a strong need to build and be part of a wider community.

This will become increasingly evident in the Month of February. You have your goals, you have worked hard all Month, but now you recognise that you can't do it all alone, (and why would you want to), you begin searching for like minded souls, your own 'Tribe' to be part of, to learn and grow with.

Take care to speak with compassion and kindness this Month. Let go of any residual anger of the past. Breathe through the change that is occurring. Relax and know you are guided.

Throat concerns may appear due to a resistance to communicate how you truly feel.

Affirmation for February

"*I trust that I am guided. I speak with kindness, compassion and love to those in my past, those in my present and those in my future. I trust the Universes process. I am exactly where I need to be. My true love is attracted to me on every level. I am loved*".

Read energy of Number 2 for more insight.

March - 03 energy

Like the energy of number 3, March brings with it the energy of Faith, Wealth & understanding our relationship with both.

You may be tested this Month on a personal level. Trust is needed. Faith that you are on the right path, that you are doing what you need to move forward, to grow, to evolve.

With great change comes great resistance. You may feel that especially this Month.

This is the Month to know you are guided.

There will be dark nights of the Soul, but know that a healing is taking place from the work you have done up till now. Breathe through it. Relax in it. Try not to push through it. Just allow it to flow around you.

Use the Law of Attraction when it seems that your Faith is beginning to wane.

Know that what you desired has already arrived.

Affirmation for March

"I trust in the Law of Attraction. My feelings match my desire. I know that I am guided. I breathe in to the new energy without resistance. I am home here. I am safe here. I am needed here. I am loved and loving in this space. Everything I desire has already arrived. I accept all this and better".

Read energy of Number 3 for more insight.

April - 04 energy

Stability arrives this Month after all the hard work you have done in the previous 3 months. Strong foundations need to be put in place if you are to move forward towards your destined achievements.

A letting go of that which no longer serves you and an embrace of new energy is needed.

You are being asked to help others this Month. Use the strength in your own Faith to allow others to succeed.

A stepping away from negative Father energy.

Let go and know that you are loved.

Do not fear your own strength, rather, embrace it, celebrate it, feel it course through your being, this energy, this is what creates momentous achievements.

This is what's needed this Month.

Stepping stones, new pathways will be revealed to you.

An understanding that Nature provides the answers.

Affirmation for April

"I am strong. I am guided. Through my strength I see a clear path. I embrace change. I accept help from others. I reach out to friends and family. I have clear, loving energy that attracts loving, kind people. My bank account overflows with the energy of abundant attraction".

Read energy of Number 4 for more insight.

May - 05 energy

As with the number 5, the Month of May may either bring you joy, or bring you undone. The power to choose is all yours.

You are needing to stand up for yourself this Month. Stand for your convictions. Stand for others.

Be present in your work.

Be mindful.

Procrastination could be at a high level this Month. Recognise if that energy is around, why it is serving you.

Is it because you are achieving your goals faster than you thought possible & don't know what to do next?

Is it because you fear more change could change the way people see you?

Is it because you may feel you have let yourself done?

Remind yourself that if you persistently resist change you will always feel stuck. Change allows you to grow. Stagnation creates resentment. Letting go of the Fear. Breathe through the anxiety. Know that you are safe in your choices.

Affirmation for May

"I trust that my choices are made out of love & compassion to myself and all involved. I let go and let God. I am free to choose differently to think differently and to act differently. I am loved, loving, compassionate and kind. I attract money easily & love my adventurous life. I am exactly where I need to be and have the choice to chose differently. My strength is my truth".

Read energy of Number 5 for more insight.

June - 06 energy

This Month represents the energy of Community and connection.

It has a very strong Feminine energy.

It can be linked with the Moon & it's cycle.

It represents ebb & flow.

Give & Take.

You may find this Month that you need to compromise on what you want to attract and achieve.

Trust the Universe.

Know that if plans change, they change for a better outcome.

Resistance can creep in and you will feel roadblocks are placed before you. Know that this is all a choice. You can see them as 'roadblocks' or see them as they were intended to be viewed, as 'signposts'.

This Month you are being asked to rest. To recognise your bodies natural rhythm. Rest when you can. Work when you must. Drink water. Eat clean. Embrace Nature.

Affirmation for June

"I listen to my body for guidance. I sleep deeply and wake refreshed. I am attracted to whole foods, fruits & vegetables. I flow with the energy of life and embrace change. I accept the Universes guidance and listen always to my intuitive nature. I am whole. I am complete. I am flow".

Read energy of Number 6 for more insight.

July - 07 energy

This Month you will be tested as it is the Month of 'experience'.

If June was the energy of community and connection, and you trusted the process and attracted that which serves you abundantly you will experience great joy, laughter, happiness and a feeling of completion and knowing you are always in the right place at the right time.

Now, if last Month, you resisted change, fought your intuitive nature, isolated yourself with your thoughts, feelings and actions your experiences will teach you the lessons of trust, of faith, of asking for help, of helping others. It will teach the lessons of what you are resting again and again and again until you finally come to the conclusion that Life, the Universe & Everything always guides you, always loves you, always wants the best for you & always believes that you have the choice to choose differently.

Trust in the Universe & your life will be filled with adventure.

Mistrust the Universe & you will continue to experience fear, doubt & anxiety.

Isn't it about time you learnt to let go?

Affirmation for July

"I experience the best in life because I chose the best things for myself. I let go & trust the Universe has my back. In flowing I know that I am guided. In trusting I know that I am loved. Adventure fills my soul. Money flows to me easily & I give knowing there will always be more. Life is easy. Life is Beautiful".

Read energy of Number 7 for more insight.

August - 08 energy

Ahhh balance.

Balance is a tricky thing as we think that it is a stagnant energy.

But this is not the case.

Balance is continuously in motion. Always checking & rechecking if it needs to move slightly to find it's centre again.

This month you will find your Balance being tested.

Have you resisted change so much that you are stuck in the procrastination rut?

This Month is going to push you and pull you in every direction until you choose to become one with the balance of your Life.

The ebb & flow.

The Faith & the Trust.

August is also linked with Karmic energy.

That continual flow of give & take will be a force in your life.

Remind yourself of this: Karma is neither good nor bad. It is the continuing motion of putting the Universe back into Balance.

Love yourself.

Like yourself.

Be proud of yourself.

Praise your efforts.

Be your own cheer squad.

Stop internalising and start reaching out to friends and family.

Find you again.

Be balanced.

Affirmation for August

"I am one with Balance. I allow my Life to ebb & flow. I accept change & trust the Universe. I am guided to where I need to be. I am doing what I need to be doing. I nourish my body, mind & soul. Life loves me & I love my Life".

Read energy of Number 8 for more insight.

September - 09 energy

Are you ready to tie everything you have achieved in a tight little bow? Or have the past few months had your head spinning & you're slowly unravelling?

September is the time to sort out your life lesson once & for all.

It is the energy of number 9.

Completion.

A letting go.

A time to sort out what you need to keep & what you need to walk away from for the highest good of all involved.

September will see you truly go within & work out what your true *value* is worth.

It is the time for finances. The time for looking at the tough stuff you have been avoiding up to now & really truly being honest with yourself & with those around you.

Let it go. All of it. The only thing you need to hold on to is love. Love for yourself. YOUR SELF. Everything else will fall in to place once that occurs.

Affirmation for September

"I let go with ease. I attract only that which aligns to my true self worth. I recognise what I need to let go of. I trust the Universe. I am loved I am loving. I am always where I need to be. Life flows easily".

Read energy of Number 9 for more insight.

October - 10 energy

It is time to revaluate your position in Life.

You are being asked to understand your true gift & acknowledge that you have the power within you all along.

October's energy is strong & can be unrelenting.

Are you *still* holding on to the old stuff?

Let go of the fear & anxiety & step up into who you truly are becoming.

A metamorphosis is taking place.

Like the Butterfly inside a cocoon the more you grow the more you need to break out of your surroundings & embrace change & all that comes with it.

It is now time to shed yourself from the past & embrace the future *you*.

Understand that with this inner power comes great responsibility.

Repeat after me "Me first. Then others".

Once you recognise your inner power, your intuition will come in full force.

Trust this.

Be guided by it.

Know that whatever decisions you are making *now* your future self is thanking you for it.

Affirmation for October

"I trust the process in Life. I am all powerful. The boundaries I set for myself allow others to be attracted to my true loving self. I am always looked after. My intuition is always right. I trust. I believe in myself & the work I am here to do. I let go of fear & attract only love".

Read energy of Number 10 for more insight.

November - 11 energy

You are being asked to acknowledge the Leadership energy that you brought through as a child.

Understand that the energy of number 11 can be one of great power.

Within that power you will find a deep seeded need to connect with like minded individuals.

Your Tribe is waiting for you.

Trust your intuitive nature is guiding you to the right places at exactly the right time for your souls growth.

Fear & doubt may come to you this month as you step forward on a new path.

Trust this.

Know that you are never given lessons in life that you yourself can not work through.

Affirmation for November

"I acknowledge my ancestors & those that have passed before me. I am being guided. I step forward in to my future with excitement. Everything is easy. I no longer feel pain of the past. My future is bright. Money is attracted to me. I have everything I need right now".

Read energy of Number 11 for more insight.

December - 12 energy

A new beginning is taking place & you are being asked to recognise the power of your own voice.

Like the numbers 1 & 2, you are being shown that you, as an individual, have the power to shape your future *IF* you trust in your own inner guidance & speak with a loving heart.

Know that words have power.

Your words have power.

They can hurt or they can heal.

Recognise that within the words you say is the feelings attached to the past.

Have you fully let go of past hurts?

Have you fully forgiven yourself & those that have hurt you?

It is time now to trust that you are moving in to a new life.

Step confidently towards your dreams, your goals.

See yourself in the future & then *feel* what that feels like.

That is the way of abundance.

That is the way to attracting what you truly desire.

Trust it.

Feel it. Then let it go & allow Life, The Universe & Everything to move Heaven & Earth to bring those things to you.

Let go of judgement.

Affirmation for December

"I forgive & am forgiven. I speak only with loving words, to myself & to others. I trust the process of Life. I walk confidently into the future knowing I am enough. I have enough. I am always guided. I am always loved. In loving I am loved. In forgiving I am forgiven".

Read energy of Number 12 for more insight.

One last thing…

Remember always, that you have the power to choose a different life , a different lesson, a different path.

You have the power all along.

Not your family, not your friends, not society.

You.

And right now, *we need you*.

We need you to trust yourself & the path that has been chosen for you & by you.

We need you to stand up for us, & speak up on our behalf.

We need you to shake off the fear & anxiety that you have chosen to hang on to for far too long & step in to your true power.

This is your signpost.

Let intuition be your guide.

Trust yourself & know that you are loved.

xoxoNickib

Have you loved this book?
I would love to hear from you!
Come say Hi at fb.com/Nickibtv

Want to work with me? I specialising in helping Women climb the ladder to Social Media success 1 step at a time by creating digital courses, free daily content, private membership & 1 on 1 training.

Find out more at socialvibetribe.com

Write a review on Amazon & Goodreads to share with others what you loved.

Chapter 9. About Nicole:

Nicole Suzanne Brown lives her life between sunny Queensland and Düsseldorf Germany. Small in stature but big in personality, she has lived in Germany, New York, the United Kingdom, spent time in an Indian Ashram and gets itchy feet every time she glances at her Passport.

She is the founder of Social Vibe Tribe where she specialises in helping Women climb the ladder to Social Media success. And a 6 day a week vlogger at Nickibtv where she helps Women create a positive mindset in life & business.

She is the Author of Passing through Time – conversations with the other side, The Creativity Workbook, The Wee Little Book of The Awesome, The Meaning of Feathers, The Meaning of Numbers, and the Fictions: Pride and soon to be released Outback Mistress (2019), and Phoenix (2019).

Her digital courses include
Go LIVE Like a PRO - 18page digital workbook to take the fear out of going live on Facebook.

Be a Freakin' Lighthouse - 22page digital workbook to help find your ideal client on social media.

When not writing you can find her with her Wife Anne-Marie contemplating their navels, somewhere, in some part of the world.

Other works by Nicole Suzanne Brown

The Meaning of Feathers

In this 118page book you will learn:
Feathers and Flight – What it all means.
The Spiritual and Physical Meaning of Feathers.
Feathers and The Body – How they affect your physical and spiritual bodies.
Feather colours and their Physical/Spiritual Meanings.
How the number of feathers can mean something unique.
Tune in and Tune out with Feathers – How to Meditate with the Feather that you have found.
What does finding a Feather mean?
What does a Black Feather mean?
What does it mean when you find a Feather in your house?
The information in this book is for you to learn, grow, express and create your own pathway to your own spirituality.

Whether you have been walking on your spiritual path for eons of time or just tipped forward on your path.

The information received was out of a need, and urge to learn more about what Feathers mean, and why they sometimes magically appear.

Are they here to teach us something about ourselves?

Can Feathers hold messages for us, that can unlock healing and change?

Can they help with creativity and bring messages form beyond time and space?

I believe they can.

I believe they do.

And by the end of this book, you will too.

Reviews for The Meaning of Feathers

5 Stars
Well worth every penny spent! Well written! Very accurate! I found this book very helpful! I searched the internet high and low and could not find the information I needed to receive the messages from the feathers that was sent by my angels that I kept finding and this book was the only resource I could find! This book is just what I needed in order to receive the divine guidance that I was meant to receive!
Andrea - Amazon Customer

5 Stars
This was a gift for a feather lover and collector and she said it was one of the best, she had read.
- Amazon Customer

5 Stars
Such a well written book I just loved it and I will use it a lot
I love reading about the meaning of feathers
Elisa - Amazon Customer

The Creativity Workbook - kindle only

The Creativity Workbook will give you what tips, tricks and secrets I used to go from a frumpy life to one of fabulous creativity and wealth.
You will learn:
How to push through procrastination and love your life.
How I lost my mojo then found it all over again.
Affirmations, how to's & secrets galore! Testimonial ...

PLUS! Included in the Creativity Workbook you receive the TA-DA! LIST - (To Do lists are so yesterday).

Use your FREE TA-DA List & be proud every day of what you have accomplished.

Available on Amazon Kindle Only

The Wee Little Book of The Awesome

Create the life you want to live by manifesting and pulling from the Universe the experiences you want!

In this 16 page pdf you will learn:
Why it is sooo important to Breathe.
Why it is sooo important to Love yourself & put yourself first.

The Meaning of Numbers — Nicole Suzanne Brown

Why it is sooo important to celebrate EVERY SINGLE DAY!

Available on Amazon Kindle only

Passing through Time

(conversations with the other side)

Jason was a strong, fit and healthy young man with everything to look forward to in life.

His death of a heart attack at 29 years of age was a sudden shock to his loved ones. It was a short time later that he started to communicate with his sister Nicole. Jason explains to his sister what he saw when he died, or as he calls it "Passing through Time". Jason describes the feelings of overwhelming peace and love that you experience when you pass through time, as well as what others experience (children, car accident victims, etc.)Jason also speaks about how we can naturally heal the human body through positive affirmation and meditation, Angels, Forgiveness, the energy of God, and the energy of pure Love that is available to us all.

Reviews for Passing Through Time:

"**Passing Through Time** is 'conversations with God' on a more intimate, realistic scale.

A lot of questions one might pose to God, or what we as mortal humans have perhaps considered inwardly, quietly to ourselves, Nicole openly asks her brother Jason, who has passed away in the prime of his life. He tells Nicole his own personal spiritual life experiences from 'the other side'. Nicole shows no fear in communicating with Jason, I would be a little uncomfortable in the same situation. However, she is perfectly comfortable sensing Jason's presence.

I love that Jason indicates to Nicole that life is the 'illusion', and death a kind of 'reality'. Regardless whether or not you believe in life after death, it's an interesting take on the philosophy of life.

Nicole cleverly interspersed the stark reality of Jason's sudden death via short takes from her Mum's diary. A humbling reminder of the other side of death, that whilst Jason is happy and content, those left behind are struggling.

An enlightening read. Comforting and reassuring, no matter which side of the fence you sit on regarding your own personal beliefs on the big question, does life after death exist?"

Aishah Macgill, co-founder of Australian Writers Rock

"Nicole Brown's book – "Passing through Time" is a beautiful breath of fresh Energy. It encapsulates Spiritual Philosophy and Spiritual Truths succinctly, and in such a way that really guides the reader through what may otherwise be very esoteric information. It was like re-connecting with a very wise friend. A Must-Read for anyone wanting to understand the Spiritual Dimensions of Life – this One and the Next!"

Donna Nelson

www.TheSpiritualAdventuresOf.com

5 Stars
I could not put this book down. I found the questions asked were the answers I was looking for....My favorite was the very last one answered. Loved this book!
Sue - Amazon Customer

5 Stars

I have only read the 16% part of the book,enough that I am going to love the entire book. Love lives on and we will always have our loved ones in our life. It made me realize that communication comes in many forms. Thank you

Nicole for sharing your book.
Man - Amazon Customer

Chapter one
Passing Through Time
Conversations with the Other Side
Introduction

Jason was strong, fit and healthy. His death at age 29 of a heart attack on 20th December, 1998, came as a sudden shock to myself, my parents and his fiancé Gaylene (just engaged the day he died).

Through remembrance of his love for us all and mine for him, we began speaking to each other shortly after his death.

The following conversations of his adventures and remembrances of passing through time gave us all great comfort and helped us live through our loss and sadness. He continues to communicate with me, and has taught me about what it is like to die, or as he chooses to call it 'Pass through Time'. Revelations of love, truth and peace-filled existence of the after-life is evident in his learning's and memories.

His and my only wish is for all of us not to fear 'death' or have fears for the loved ones that have passed 'before' us, but to remember and

reconnect with each other through the love we share.

Nicole 2012

'I'm so happy now Mum.
I've found my purpose'
Jason 16/12/98

First Conversation with Jason

The feelings of grief cannot be explained in layman's terms. For every single person it is an individual experience.

Some get angry, others remorseful. But, the most important thing for anyone, everyone, is that they feel every feeling to its full extent.

The first conversation I had with Jay was only days after he passed. Days for us, a lifetime for him. I was lying on his bed, listening to his favourite song, consumed with grief, confusion, heartbroken and lonely. I kept asking why? Why him, why now? When there were so many nasty people in the world, why 'take' him? I questioned GOD. I questioned every belief I had. And in that questioning with my own thoughts raging in my head, I heard him.

I will never publish the first conversation that we had. It was deeply personal. Messages for family and friends, loving memories that he had for each of us and only us. But in that first conversation we connected through time, through energy and through the love we have for each other.

It's so important to be connected right now with the ones you love.

Tell them how deeply you feel; tell them how grateful you are that they are who they are. Let them know that no matter what happens, not matter where you are in the world you *will* connect. Oceans apart or eons apart. You will always be connected.

Our family did that in the last phone call we had with Jay only hours before he passed.

We kept our promise.

We now hope we can teach you to make and keep yours.

Nicole 2012.

My Son is dead.

My heart is breaking and my Son is dead.

Journal entry - 21/12/98

Mum

Jason's Experience

Jay, what did dying feel like? So many people are so terrified of death. And I think it's the 'not knowing' that scares the crap out of everyone, even the most resilient.

For me personally, because everyone's experience of passing is different 'as is their life, so is their death' it was the most peaceful thing I have ever felt.

I remember laughing with Gaylene and making plans for our wedding and also our future. I remember lying there and talking with her with the lights out and I held her hand when I was falling asleep.

Then I remembered that I had this feeling of total peacefulness, it was like I was finally complete. I was grateful for all that struggle in my life to get me right here to this place right now. I knew where I was going in life, who I was, where I finally fitted in. I guess I had never really done that before - given thanks, been grateful, truly grateful for all that I have and don't have. I was grateful for the woman lying next to me, for

Mum, Dad and you. My friends; for all that I received and had, I 'knew' who I was, finally. It's like I got it! I found the last piece of the puzzle, the clue to the riddle. I worked out the meaning of life.

The Meaning of Numbers   Nicole Suzanne Brown

I remember saying 'If this is the happiest I am ever going to be'…

Then …

… I was outside of myself, looking over Gaylene and I sleeping. I was lying on my stomach with my leg off to one side. There were all these colors around me. At first I thought they were all around me and then I noticed the colors were around everything.

It's amazing Nicole. Every time I breathed in, the colours changed to brighter vibrant colors. Then every time I breathed out, they become pastel colors, still vibrant but not as bright. I remember lifting my hand up and watching the gold light like a wave, going not only around my hand, but through it as well. When I breathed in, things like objects became denser and when I breathed back out, they were shimmery, like a wave, like heat on a road. I guess that's how they explain energy. I remembered thinking this is what astral travelling is probably like.

I remember looking around the room and 'pushing' the colors with my hands. The colors moved and glided. They didn't crash into each other or become jagged or fragmented.

The Meaning of Numbers — Nicole Suzanne Brown

They danced and gelled into each other, separating and then coming back together again. I'd never seen anything like it on Earth, but I just knew it was right. I wasn't scared or nervous I was excited and knew that that's how life was, always. That's how it is and we just don't see it.

I then looked more closely at my face.

I remember thinking and feeling that it looked so grey and old, when all I felt was really young and fit. I guess you could say it was that I felt alive for the first time in my life. Really alive. Free. When I was looking at myself, it all began to change.

I realized when I breathed in I could see everything inside me, my lungs and my bones, my skeleton and my heart. I looked over at

Gaylene and could see the same thing, her lungs going in and out with every breath she took and her heart beating. I smiled at her 'cause she looked so beautiful and peaceful. I looked back at myself again, lying there beside her and noticed something was different.

It took me a while I guess, looking back and forth from myself to Gaylene when it dawned on me.

My lungs weren't moving and my heart wasn't beating like hers. It wasn't beating at all.

When I realized what that meant, I thought for a second that I should feel scared. I tried to and waited for the panic and fear to rise inside me...but it never came. I sat there for what seemed a long time, just looking at myself.

Looking at my body, my face ...

... And then I began to cry. Not because I was sad or scared, but because I wasn't. I knew what it all meant. I had died. It was sudden and not at all like I thought I would die. But I knew that I had left time behind for the last time. I was free. I didn't feel sad or frustrated or worthless. I didn't feel that struggle or fight to be good or funny or liked. I didn't feel anything negative at all. Just peaceful. Only peace.

After a while of sitting there, I wiped the tears from my eyes and looked down at them on my hands. My tears had now become gold light and energy. I remember thinking 'so that's what pure love looks like'.

I looked up and all the colors around me had become really bright and vibrated. Then through the colors came these people, or Beings of Light I suppose you would call them. And they were smiling at me. I remember looking at the Beings and shrugged my shoulders at them.

Not like a 'well, what's next?' thing, but a 'So, this is it' thing.

They nodded as if they knew what I was thinking, and then they smiled at me and came closer.

It's funny to remember it now, but when you look at these Beings, their appearance changes to whatever or whoever you think about. The first thing I thought of was 'will I see Charlie Brown?' - our childhood dog. Isn't that funny?

Then suddenly there he was, this being changed instantly into Charlie Brown and he came bounding up to me. I laughed and cried as I held him cause he was exactly how I remembered him.

I then thought of White Feather - my spirit guide and another Being changed into him instantly. He was a lot taller than I thought he would be and I guess the surprised look on my face is what made him laugh. As soon as we touched all the memories we had shared together over our lifetimes with him came flooding back, especially the times in this life, when I thought I had no-one, I could see now that he was there, standing behind me with his hand on my shoulder like he was just then.

I then thought of your spirit guide Nicole - Soaring Eagle and White Feather instantly changed his appearance to look like your guide, or how I imagined him to look - (I'll talk to you more about that later). I thought of Mum's guide and again the face and the body of the Being changed.

The Meaning of Numbers — Nicole Suzanne Brown

I must have thought something because I suddenly heard in my head that 'WE ARE ALL ONE - ALL PART OF EACH OTHER'

I thought of Grandad and Uncle Terry and Aunty Gloria and these Beings came through the colors and changed into them.

We all laughed and hugged each other. Uncle Terry looked really healthy, really young like I remembered him when we used to go fishing, or over at his place where we played pool. I must have started thinking of a lot of people then, because more and more Beings changed appearance to look like who I was thinking of. I even thought of Peter Allen - the singer - I don't know why; and he came in front of me. Now, HE'S a lot shorter than I thought he would be (laughs). I then thought of you, Mum and Dad and looked back around to see myself lying there again. Beings changed into you, Mum and Dad and everyone I thought of that wasn't dead.

For a split second, I couldn't understand why.

Then as soon as I thought about it the answer came.

The Meaning of Numbers — Nicole Suzanne Brown

'There is no time'. Our lives truly are instant Nicole. What we see as a 'lifetime' really is just a blink of an eye or a single breath.

You and Mum and Dad and I all hugged and the memories of our lives together came flooding back, things I thought I had forgotten were instantly relived and we laughed and cried and I was once again thankful for having the life I had shared with you all.

I looked over at Gaylene and she began to wake up. I was concerned for her, although that 'feeling' didn't come over me - just the thought. I heard her telling me to roll over because she thought I was snoring. She then touched me and I saw my body go all stiff like an ironing board. It was like all my muscles went into spasm. She then jumped out of bed, ran over to turn on the light, and then was at my side rolling me over. She stepped back for a moment because my eyes were wide open. Then she put her head to my chest, checked if I was breathing and started CPR.

Gaylene ran out of the room and called for an ambulance running back to check on me again and again trying CPR waiting for the ambulance to come. It was a strange feeling standing there viewing it all, watching her fight for my life. I thought that I would feel a pull emotionally or frightened or scared, but none of those feelings came. Then I realized something.

And in that realization I turned next to me and a Being changed into Gaylene. She was with me, the energy of her, the energy of all that I loved about her was right here with me, witnessing it all with me, being there again for me. I thanked her for fighting for my life. I thanked her for loving me in my life, I thanked her for the person she was and thanked her for the memories I will always share and have with her.

Even though all of this was only just happening it was like it happened a long time ago, like when you stub your toe, or hit your thumb with a hammer. You remember it hurt, but that's all, you just remember. The pain doesn't come with those memories; you just remember that back then, it hurt.

I don't want to dwell too much on my passing. I would rather, am here to, help you write, to remember with me, to learn and teach others about a more realistic experience of life on earth and on death, or as we like to call it 'Passing through Time'. Passing through time Nicole is an adventure, a mystery, an answer to the unknown that Western civilization (myself included), search for all their lives.

It is a plausible realization of the GOD-Force, GOD-Self in all of us.

It is energy.

It is pure love.

It is a fantastic area of life that we have closed the door on for so long; we forgot the great adventure it holds.

The realization of the Human Spirit is upon us. In your lifetime you will grasp your dreams, live your dreams in reality.

That is all we want, isn't it? Hopefully with these writings, people will begin to not search for the meaning of life but instead live and 'Be' their answer, only striving for them 'selves' the essence of who they really are.

I will tell you of great things, unbelievable sights and realizations as I come upon them and them upon me. This is my calling I have found my way.

Allow me to teach you to find yours.

Jason.

Jay, several times throughout these communications you have stated that 'when you take your first breath when you pass'. Does that mean you breathe after death? (I hear Jay breathe in and out and then 'feel' his shoulders shrug).

Yeah, I guess so. I never really thought about it. But then again, how many times on Earth do you actually 'think' about breathing.

Remember, life is the illusion. Passing through time is the reality.

Can you feel?

Absolutely! The feelings are intensified to such a rapid vibration that all you do is feel. As I just explained, when communicating here and with you, feeling is everything. There is nothing separate or apart from that essence of energy.

I feel such love, more than I ever felt capable of or knew even existed. I feel peace, joy, excitement, anticipation, love for you all and also love for myself. Some here do feel anger or bitterness, but once they realize the energy that surrounds them, is them, they move rapidly into the energy of peace and love, that is just the energy of learning and remembrance.

Do you have a body that you are aware of?

When you pass, initially you have the 'thought' of the body that you did when you were on earth because it is comfortable and familiar.

Then when you become accustomed and used to the energy around you, you notice a change in your physical self. You become lighter and less dense in your energy. You become more luminescent with your surroundings. You can call energy into your being until you realize that that's just what you are already - intellectual energy.

You begin to vibrate at a more rapid vibrational structure than you ever could on Earth. Therefore there is no need for such a dense vibrational form as a 'physical' body.

I can still be in the form of 'Jason' whenever I want or choose to be. The energy vibration of that intellect is just remembering or oscillating at a more defined or higher vibration molecularly. I like this form and these memories. I suppose you can say I'm just a mere shadow of my former self (laughs).

When I speak to you I am able to remember or re-invent the molecular structure of 'Jason' because you are used to that energy.

You are comfortable with it. You are accustomed to it. You are also, importantly, connected to that particular vision of the energy I oscillate with. Now, by using the energy and becoming one with it, I am able, if I feel like it, to transcend my energy to an energy level outside of the physical form. We all do it, here and where you are. Although you call it 'dream state/astral travel'. Same thing. Now, when we greet people who have passed and say their individual Prayer of Remembrance, we come in light form or 'light bodies'- bodies of light. That's what I saw when I passed and now I am one of them when other's pass. It seems to help the person passing through to 'remember' who they are and why they are.

The light that we emit is a remembrance and a resurgence of peacefilled love moving at a slightly higher vibration to that of Earth.

You're kind of eased into the realization of remembrance. The energy then moves them to a particular energy- based realized form. We are all part of ourselves.

Have you any depth of the physical? Can you touch, smell etc?

Again, of course. Remember, the physical is the illusion. There on Earth, we use only 12% of our brain or intellect some even less (laughs).

The only reason that humans have the 'lower' intellect of remembrance is just that; they have forgotten their remembrance of the intellect.

Once humans establish a re-connection with their own vibration, their intellect then grows or oscillates at a higher more rapid energy. You are able to access more because, in remembrance, your intellect opens more to new ideas and growth 'spurts'. I am able to touch, smell, hear and see etc,. as I did on Earth, but again, at a more rapid molecular structure. I can also touch, hear, smell and see you in your own molecular structure. The touch you receive feels sometimes like a feather has brushed your face or hands.

Depending on the energy you are oscillating at, at a particular time, the touch may become stronger. Being in touch with your loved ones, connecting so strongly through thought, feeling, love and remembrance allows the boundaries to be lifted and the energy to flow freely. Your energy connecting with mine is through the energy of remembrance so you are able to 'receive' more senses. In those circumstances, the touch will become more direct - like someone poking you in the eye, sticking their finger in your ear, pulling your hair, or taps on the shoulder etc,.

It is in the energy of connection of remembrance that allows us all to communicate with each other, everywhere. Heaven literally on Earth. Hopefully with our conversations, the people will begin to open their collective thoughts just enough to allow that to happen. More people especially in the western world seeking communication openly and lovingly will allow energy to move and evolve. Conflicts will lessen and love will shine through. Learning's of spirituality will be honored and taught from cradle to grave. Openly without fear, without boundaries. Eastern teachings know this, yet the western world is still lost, still confused, still feels alone and isolated.

Passing Through Time - Conversations with the Other Side available through both Amazon, Kindle

Fiction novels also by Nicole Suzanne Brown

Outback Mistress (2019)

"A wayward sister returns to her homestead, only to find her brother, a highly decorated Police Officer murdered, and the entire town acting suspiciously.".

CHAPTER 1.

Living in a small Country town is not for the faint hearted. Even though Portland is not your typical town, there isn't the growing space for mediocrity. You either fit in or move out. It's that simple. With its tiny butter box houses, littered out front with planter boxes of pansies and lavender, neighbours who have been friends since kindergarten sit on their front porch swings, lazily waving their hands across their faces to shoo away the sticky flies, gossip over the latest rumour and chastise their children all in one sentence. Feuds between families last generations in this town even though no one knows why or how it started in the first place.

Honour is placed highly. Honour and survival. Weatherboard sheds tuck behind each house, paint split and curling in the harsh heat and bitterly cold winters. Wind willies dance along dirt laid laneways kicking up red dust, scattering across the yards, settling on the early morning washing.

The Meaning of Numbers — Nicole Suzanne Brown

Kookaburra's laughter mingles with the sounds of distant children playing against the breeze while bees gather pollen around their feet. With the Queensland floods the then drought stricken land, revived, now lush, the grass so green it hurts your eyes. The population almost halved years ago when the old cement mill shut down. Now those that stubbornly stayed, daring to see the tough times out, are firmly planted like that of the swaying willow down by Portland's creek beds.

This town was once abundant. It was incredibly affluent in every sense of the word. It was a town of wealth and business, prestige and money. It was a town of productivity and employment. It was the town that built Sydney. Those skyscrapers you see, work in, dance around to avoid the traffic in that huge Metropolitan, the townsfolk of Portland made those for you. Sydney was built with Portland cement. Its Earth is in every cell. The town of Portland is in its D.N.A. It breathes because of this town. It grows now because of Portland's foundation.

It is a strong town. A proud town. Full of strong personalities and an ever beating heart. When the Cement works closed it felt like the breath was sucked out too. The riches and abundance left the town. Only the strong survived. Those that remembered.

Those that never gave up hope that one day the town would turn around, but after a decade the town now is now lost, counting on one hand the businesses that have stayed open and struggle each week to do so.

Nothing much happens here. The odd domestic disturbance when the welfare cheque runs out and the alcohol dares to run low. A few drunken disorderly misdemeanors when one of the young men turn 18, many more when an old farmer dies from self inflicted injuries. With one grocery store, connected to the pub, a school that hosts kindergarten to high school, and a large graveyard on the outskirts of town, several large cattle properties nestle amongst the hills, there wasn't much that Matthew Noble couldn't keep an eye on. He runs his hands through his short cropped hair; adjusts his gun belt on his hip and leans back against the bar.

The pub was busy, and Matthew Noble was happy that they were all in one place at the one time so he could keep an eye on them. Having returned back to the homestead a fully decorated police officer years before, he loved the quiet paced energy of the town compared to the rat race of Sydney. The generosity and individuality of the town folk that jostle and laugh around him excited to be spending his Birthday welcomed him back to the fold; more so now that he shouted the last two rounds. He was, in the eyes of the small community, a top bloke.

The Meaning of Numbers   Nicole Suzanne Brown

He watches the clock that hangs precariously above the fireplace and counts down the seconds till it chimes eleven times. He figured an hour out of his night shift was enough to be seen as being seen, but he needed to also make a quiet exit so he didn't cramp anyone's style, let alone his own.

Marv Grainer lazily leans against the bar allowing his beer gut to hang on the lower shelf. A huge man with small stature, he kept the alcohol flowing and the bar tabs to a minimum. He had inherited the bar from his father and his before him. Late at night when the bar is empty and the drunkards have all staggered home, he fires up sing star opera and dreams of a time when he could have done whatever he wanted with his life. Yet he knew dreams and wishes are for fools and you have to work with what you've been given. He catches a glimpse of Matthew heading towards the exit and bellows over the conversations of the patrons. "Matt! Come on mate! My shout this time..!" Matthew waves his hand no, following with a thumbs up sign and steps out to the cold night air. "Piker" Marv grunts pushing back a young cowhand shaking his empty schooner glass in his face "Not you, ya fucknut"

The night air's crisp clean smell is quickly replaced by the harsh green coal smoke that lingers above all the houses around town. The town is frugal with their money with no sense or compassion for environmental damage their warm houses cause. Matthew sniffs and clears his throat, shrugging his coat up closely to cover his neck. He strides over to his patrol car, pulling his key out of his pocket.

Lisa Muller stands on the balcony eyeing Matthew with interest. Dressed in low cut second-hand lingerie, she is a tiny girl, with straight blonde hair down to her waist, a bubbly personality and the town's jezebel. Of course ask any man in this town and they will emphatically deny it. The women, however, will not. She leans over the rail and purrs sweet and low "Happy Birthday Handsome" Matthew stops short turning to look up. He has known her since grade school, was her first kiss, and knew she had a sweet spot for him, as he did her, but never really grew too attached to her. He never really grew too attached to anyone, except for his homestead and the land that surrounds it. He touches the brim of his Police baseball cap and smiles shyly "Thank you Lisa, I appreciate that". She smiles big and nods back towards her bedroom "Don't feel like coming in for a little celebration do you?" He shakes his head and smiles up at her causing her heart to do a double beat while her stomach flip flops. He shakes his head no "I'm all partied out, but thank you tho". Lisa pouts playfully "Oh, I'm sure we can find something else to do to keep each other entertained" Matthew looks down and scuffs his shoe against the dirt plastered on his front tyre. "I'm sure we could Lisa. Maybe some other time. Thank you again tho. You have a good night. Keep safe now".

Lisa swoons "Matthew, you are such a polite, sweet thing, someone's going to take advantage of that someday. Maybe even me" Matthew laughs up at her "Maybe Lisa. Night."

She watches his strong shoulders and tight arse get into the car and wishes her life was so very much different to what she was living right now.

She closes her eyes, momentarily drowning out the snoring patron sprawled on her bed behind her, clothes and a gun belt strewn over her lounge and floor and dreams of simpler, happier times.

Justin, a pimpled skin, skinny man poking his head out of the front door of the pub yells up at her, breaking her out of her daydream "Hey Lisa! Why don't we do something different tonight and you pay me?" Lisa's good mood vanishes like coal smoke on a winter's breeze, She flinches, shows him her middle finger and steps back through her glittered nylon curtains, back to the daydream, far away from here. Justin is jostled back to the bar, his voice gruff "What is it with that woman, with men in uniform?" he slumps at the bar and taps his glass for a refill "I'm sure a lot of women would find sanitation worker's uniforms attractive mate" Marv slides the beer over to him, stopping expertly in front of the saddened sanitary worker. He sulks into his beer "They only want you if something's stuck-up or needs plunging" Marv snorts, "You should be more popular then mate!"

The Meaning of Numbers   Nicole Suzanne Brown

Matthew, hands on hips, stands on the side of a dirt road on the outskirts of town, staring down at his back tyre now flat and shredded to the rim. For the last half hour he has driven slowly through the town streets and past properties making sure all those who are not still at the pub are tucked tightly and safely in their homes.

He kicks the tyre with his foot, takes his cap off, scratches the back of his head, walks around to the back of the car popping the boot, pulling out the tyre jack and spare tyre. He plonks himself down on the spare tyre and goes to work loosening the wheel nuts.

A Ute slowly drives towards Matthew, tyres scrunching over the dry dirt road stopping short just meters away, high beams piercing through the darkness. The driver jumps down from the car. Matthew squints, shielding his eyes from the glare of the lights. He instantly recognises the driver approaching. He leans back on his heels and points at his tyre. "Well hello stranger, long time no see. Can you believe my luck? Tonight of all nights." He turns back to loosen the last wing nut "What you doing out this way?"

A single gunshot echoes across the still night; Matthew falls awkwardly to the ground, eyes wide open in shock, a single trickle of blood runs from his left ear. The driver nudges Matthews's body with their soiled stained work boot, turns and walks back to his vehicle.

The Ute roars to life, driving slowly past Matthew's lifeless body, shifts gears as tyres spin spewing dirt and dust behind it.

For further updates, pre-orders & awesomeness visit Nicole at Social Vibe Tribe and her facebook profile Nickibtv.

Nickibtv as well as her Amazon author page.

www.ingramcontent.com/pod-product-compliance
Lightning Source LLC
Chambersburg PA
CBHW070431010526
44118CB00014B/1995